Demeter by Robert Seymour Bridges

WRITTEN FOR THE LADIES AT SOMERVILLE COLLEGE & ACTED BY THEM AT THE INAUGURATION OF THEIR NEW BUILDING IN 1904

Robert Bridges was born in Walmer, Kent on the 23rd of October 1844. He went to study medicine intending to practice until the age of forty and then retire to write poetry.

Lung disease forced him to retire in 1882, and from that point on he devoted himself to writing and literary research. However, Bridges' literary work started long before his retirement, his first collection of poems having been published in 1873.

He was appointed Poet Laureate in 1913 by George V, the only medical graduate to have held the office.

He died in Oxford on the 21st of April 1930.

Index of Contents

A Mask

"Dreams & the light imaginings of men"

ARGUMENT OF THE PLAY

The scene is in the flowery valley below Enna. Hades prologizes, and tells how he has come with consent of Zeus to carry off Persephone to be his queen. The Chorus of Ocean nymphs entering praise Sicily and the spring. Persephone enters with Athena and Artemis to gather flowers for the festival of Zeus. Persephone being left alone is carried off by Hades.

In the second act, which is ten days later, the Chorus deplore the loss of Persephone. Demeter entering upbraids them in a choric scene and describes her search for Persephone until she learnt her fate from Helios. Afterwards she describes her plan for compelling Zeus to restore Hermes. Hermes brings from Zens a command to Demeter that she shall return to Olympus. She sends defiance to Zeus, and the Chorus end the scene by vowing to win Poseidon to aid Demeter.

In the third act, which is a year later, the Chorus, who have been summoned by Demeter to witness the restoration of Persephone, lament Demeter's anger. Demeter narrates the Eleusinian episode of her wanderings, until Hermes enters leading Persephone. After their greeting Demeter hears from Hermes the terms of Persephone's restoration; she is reconciled thereto by Persephone, and invites her to Eleusis. The Chorus sing and crown Persephone with flowers.

DRAMATIS PERSONÆ
HADES.
DEMETER.
PERSEPHONE.
ATHENA.
ARTEMIS.
HERMES.
Chorus of OCEANIDES.

DEMETER

HADES

I am the King of Hell, nor prone to vex
Eternal destiny with weak complaint;
Nor when I took my kingdom did I mourn
My lot, from heav'n expell'd, deny'd to enjoy
Its radiant revelry and ambrosial feast,
Nor blamed our mighty Sisters, that not one
Would share my empire in the shades of night.
But when a younger race of gods arose,
And Zeus set many sons on heav'nly seats,
And many daughters dower'd with new domain,
And year by year were multiply'd on earth
Their temples and their statu'd sanctities,
Mirrors of man's ideas that grow apace,
Yea, since man's mind was one with my desire
That Hell should have a queen,—for heav'n hath queens
Many, nor on all earth reigns any king
In unkind isolation like to me,—
I claimed from Zeus that of the fair immortals
One should be given to me to grace my throne.
Willing he was, and quick to praise my rule,
And of mere justice there had granted me
Whome'er I chose: but 'Brother mine,' he said,
'Great as my power among the gods, this thing
I cannot compass, that a child of mine,
Who once hath tasted of celestial life,
Should all forgo, and destitute of bliss
Descend into the shades, albeit to sit

An equal on thy throne. Take whom thou wilt;
But by triumphant force persuade, as erst
I conquer'd heav'n.' Said I 'My heart is set:
I take Demeter's child Persephone;
Dost thou consent?' Whereto he gave his nod.
And I am come to-day with hidden powers,
Ev'n unto Enna's fair Sicilian field,
To rob her from the earth. 'Tis here she wanders
With all her train: nor is this flow'ry vale
Fairer among the fairest vales of earth,
Nor any flower within this flow'ry vale
Fair above other flowers, as she is fairest
Among immortal goddesses, the daughter
Of gentle-eyed Demeter; and her passion
Is for the flowers, and every tenderness
That I have long'd for in my fierce abodes.
But she hath always in attendant guard
The dancing nymphs of Ocean, and to-day
The wise Athena and chaste Artemis
Indulge her girlish fancy, gathering flowers
To deck the banner of my golden brother,
Whose thought they guess not, tho' their presence here
Affront his will and mine. If once alone
I spy her, I can snatch her swiftly down:
And after shall find favour for my fault,
When I by gentle means have won her love.
I hear their music now. Hither they come:
I'll to my ambush in the rocky cave.

ACT I

Enter CHORUS OF OCEANIDES, with baskets.

OCEANIDES
Gay and lovely is earth, man's decorate dwelling;
With fresh beauty ever varying hour to hour.
As now bathed in azure joy she awakeneth
With bright morn to the sun's life-giving effluence,
Or sunk into solemn darkness aneath the stars
In mysterious awe slumbereth out the night,
Then from darkness again plunging again to day;
Like dolphins in a swift herd that accompany
Poseidon's chariot when he rebukes the waves.
But no country to me 'neath the enarching air
Is fair as Sicily's flowery fruitful isle:
Always lovely, whether winter adorn the hills

With his silvery snow, or generous summer
Outpour her heavy gold on the river-valleys.
Her rare beauty giveth gaiety unto man,
A delite dear to immortals.

2

And one season of all chiefly deliteth us,
When fair Spring is afield. O happy is the Spring!
Now birds early arouse their pretty minstreling;
Now down its rocky hill murmureth ev'ry rill;
Now all bursteth anew, wantoning in the dew
Their bells of bonny blue, their chalices honey'd.
Unkind frost is away; now sunny is the day;
Now man thinketh aright, Life it is all delite.
Now maids playfully dance o'er enamel'd meadows,
And with goldy blossom deck forehead and bosom;
While old Pan rollicketh thro' the budding shadows,
Voicing his merry reed, laughing aloud to lead
The echoes madly rejoicing.

3

We be Oceanids, Persephone's lovers,
Who all came hurrying joyfully from the sea
Ere daybreak to obey her belovëd summons.
At her fancy to pluck these violets, lilies,
Windflow'rs and daffodils, all for a festival
Whereat shé will adorn Zeuses honour'd banner.
And with Persephone there cometh Artemis
And grave Pallas ... Hilloo! Already they approach!
Haste, haste! Stoop to gather! Seem busy ev'ryone!
Crowd all your wicker arcs with the meadow-lilies;
Lest our disreverenc'd deity should rebuke
The divine children of Ocean.

[Enter ATHENA, PERSEPHONE, and ARTEMIS. Persephone has a basket half fill'd with gather'd flowers.]

ATHENA
These then are Enna's flowery fields, and here
In midmost isle the garden of thy choice?

PERSEPHONE
Is not all as I promist? Feel ye not
Your earthborn ecstasy concenter'd here?
Tell me, Athena, of thy wisdom, whénce

Cometh this joy of earth, this penetrant
Palpitant exultation so unlike
The balanc't calm of high Olympian state?
Is't in the air, the tinted atmosphere
Whose gauzy veil, thrown on the hills, will paint
Their features, changing with the gradual day,
Rosy or azure, clouded now, and now
Again afire? Or is it that the sun's
Electric beams—which shot in circling fans
Whirl all things with them—as they strike the earth
Excite her yearning heart, till stir'd beneath
The rocks and silent plains, she cannot hold
Her fond desires, but sends them bursting forth
In scents and colour'd blossoms of the spring?—
Breathes it not in the flowers?

ATHENA
Fair are the flowers,
Dear child; and yet to me far lovelier
Than all their beauty is thy love for them.
Whate'er I love, I contemplate my love
More than the object, and am so rejoic'd.
For life is one, and like a level sea
Life's flood of joy. Thou wond'rest at the flowers,
But I would teach thee wonder of thy wonder;
Would shew thee beauty in the desert-sand,
The worth of things unreckt of, and the truth
That thy desire and love may spring of evil
And ugliness, and that Earth's ecstasy
May dwell in darkness also, in sorrow and tears.

PERSEPHONE
I'd not believe it: why then should we pluck
The flowers and not the stalks without the flowers?

Or do thy stones breathe scent? Would not men laugh
To see the banner of almighty Zeus
Adorn'd with ragged roots and straws?—Dear Artemis,
How lovest thou the flowers?

ARTEMIS
I'll love them better
Ever for thy sake, Cora; but for me
The joy of Earth is in the breath of life
And animal motions: nor are flowery sweets
Dear as the scent of life. His petal'd cup,
What is it by the wild fawn's liquid eye
Eloquent as love-music 'neath the moon?

Nay, not a flower in all thy garden here,
Nor wer't a thousand-thousand-fold enhanc't
In every charm, but thou wouldst turn from it
To view the antler'd stag, that in the glade
With the coy gaze of his majestic fear
Faced thee a moment ere he turn'd to fly.

PERSEPHONE
But why, then, hunt and kill what thou so lovest?

ARTEMIS
Dost thou not pluck thy flowers?

PERSEPHONE
'Tis not the same.
Thy victims fly for life: they pant, they scream.

ARTEMIS
Were they not mortal, sweet, I coud not kill them.
They kill each other in their lust for life;
Nay, cruelly persecute their blemisht kin:
And they that thus are exiled from the herd
Slink heart-brok'n to sepulchral solitudes,
Defenceless and dishonour'd; there to fall
Prey to the hungry glutton of the cave,
Or stand in mute pain lingering, till they drop
In their last lair upon the ancestral bones.

PERSEPHONE
What is it that offends me?

ATHENA
'Tis Pity, child,
The mortal thought that clouds the brow of man
With dark reserve, or poisoning all delite
Drives him upon his knees in tearful prayer
To avert his momentary qualms: till Zeus
At his reiterated plaint grows wrath,
And burdens with fresh curse the curse of care.
And they that haunt with men are apt to take
Infection of his mind: thy mighty mother
Leans to his tenderness.

PERSEPHONE
How should man, dwelling
On earth that is so gay, himself be sad?
Is not earth gay? Look on the sea, the sky,
The flowers!

ATHENA

'Tis sad to him because 'tis gay.—
For whether he consider how the flowers,
—Thy miracles of beauty above praise,—
Are wither'd in the moment of their glory,
So that of all the mounting summer's wealth
The show is chang'd each day, and each day dies,
Of no more count in Nature's estimate
Than crowded bubbles of the fighting foam:
Or whether 'tis the sea, whose azure waves
Play'd in the same infinity of motion
Ages ere he beheld it, and will play
For ages after him;—alike 'tis sad
To read how beauty dies and he must die.

PERSEPHONE

Were I a man, I would not worship thee,
Thou cold essential wisdom. If, as thou say'st,
Thought makes men sorrowful, why help his thought
To quench enjoyment, who might else as I
Revel among bright things, and feast his sense
With beauty well-discern'd? Nay, why came ye
To share my pastime? Ye love not the flowers.

ATHENA

Indeed I love thee, child; and love thy flowers,—
Nor less for loving wisely. All emotions,
Whether of gods or men, all loves and passions,
Are of two kinds; they are either inform'd by wisdom,
To reason obedient,—or they are unconducted,
Flames of the burning life. The brutes of earth
And Pan their master know these last; the first
Are seen in me: betwixt the extremes there lie
Innumerable alloys and all of evil.

PERSEPHONE

Nay, and I guess your purpose with me well:
I am a child, and ye would nurse me up
A pupil in your school. I know ye twain
Of all the immortals are at one in this;
Ye wage of cold disdain a bitter feud
With Aphrodite, and ye fear for me,
Lest she should draw me to her wanton way.
Fear not: my party is taken. Hark! I'll tell
What I have chosen, what mankind shall hold
Devote and consecrate to me on earth:
It is the flowers: but only among the flowers

Those that men love for beauty, scent, or hue,
Having no other uses: I have found
Demeter, my good mother, heeds them not.—
She loves vines, olives, orchards, 'the rich leas
Of wheat, rye, barley, vetches, oats, and peas,
But for the idle flowers she hath little care:
She will resign them willingly. And think not,
Thou wise Athena, I shall go unhonour'd,
Or rank a meaner goddess unto man.
His spirit setteth beauty before wisdom,
Pleasures above necessities, and thus
He ever adoreth flowers. Nor this I guess
Where rich men only and superfluous kings
Around their palaces reform the land
To terraces and level lawns, whereon
Appointed slaves are told, to tend and feed
Lilies and roses and all rarest plants
Fetch'd from all lands; that they—these lordly men—
'Twixt flaunting avenues and wafted odours
May pace in indolence: this is their bliss;
This first they do: and after, it may be,
Within their garden set their academe:—
But in the poorest villages, around
The meanest cottage, where no other solace
Comforts the eye, some simple gaiety
Of flowers in tended garden is seen; some pinks,
Tulips, or crocuses that edge the path;
Where oft at eve the grateful labourer
Sits in his jasmin'd porch, and takes the sun:
And even the children, that half-naked go,
Have posies in their hands, and of themselves
Will choose a queen in whom to honour Spring,
Dancing before her garlanded with may.
The cowslip makes them truant, they forget
The hour of hunger and their homely feast
So they may cull the delicate primrose,
Sealing their birthright with the touch of beauty;
With unconsider'd hecatombs assuring
Their dim sense of immortal mystery.—
Yea, rich and poor, from cradle unto grave
All men shall love me, shall adore my name,
And heap my everlasting shrine with flowers.

ATHENA
Thou sayest rightly thou art a child. May Zeus
Give thee a better province than thy thought.

[Music heard.

ARTEMIS

Listen! The nymphs are dancing. Let us go!

[They move off.

Come, Cora; wilt thou learn a hunting dance?
I'll teach thee.

PERSEPHONE

Can I learn thy hunter-step
Without thy bare legs and well-buskin'd feet?

ARTEMIS

Give me thy hand.

PERSEPHONE

Stay! stay! I have left my flowers.
I follow.

[Exeunt ATHENA and ARTEMIS.

[PERSEPHONE returning to right slowly.

They understand not—Now, praise be to Zeus,
That, tho' I sprang not from his head, I know
Something that Pallas knows not.

[She has come to where her basket lies. In stooping towards it she kneels to pluck a flower: and then comes to sit on a bank with the basket in hand on her knees, facing the audience.]

Thou tiny flower!
Art thou not wise?
Who taught thee else, thou frail anemone,
Thy starry notion, thy wind-wavering motion,
Thy complex of chaste beauty, unimagin'd
Till thou art seen?—And how so wisely, thou,
Indifferent to the number of thy rays,
While others are so strict? This six-leaved tulip,
—He would not risk a seventh for all his worth,—
He thought to attain unique magnificence
By sheer simplicity—a pointed oval
Bare on a stalk erect: and yet, grown old
He will his young idea quite abandon,
In his dishevel'd fury wantoning
Beyond belief.... Some are four-leaved: this poppy
Will have but four. He, like a hurried thief,

Stuffs his rich silks into too small a bag—
I think he watch'd a summer-butterfly
Creep out all crumpled from his winter-case,
Trusting the sun to smooth his tender tissue
And sleek the velvet of his painted wings:—
And so doth he.—Between such different schemes,
Such widely varied loveliness, how choose?
Yet loving all, one should be most belov'd,
Most intimately mine; to mortal men
My emblem: tho' I never find in one
The sum of all distinctions.—Rose were best:
But she is passion's darling, and unkind
To handle—set her by.—Choosing for odour,
The violet were mine—men call her modest,
Because she hides, and when in company
Lacks manner and the assertive style of worth:—
While this narcissus here scorns modesty,
Will stand up what she is, tho' something prim:
Her scent, a saturation of one tone,
Like her plain symmetry, leaves nought to fancy:—
Whereas this iris,—she outvieth man's
Excellent artistry; elaboration
Confounded with simplicity, till none
Can tell which sprang of whiCHORUS Coud I but find
A scented iris, I should be content:
Yet men would call me proud: Iris is Pride.—
To-day I'll favour thee, sweet violet;
Thou canst live in my bosom. I'll not wrong thee
Wearing thee in Olympus.—Help! help! Ay me!

[PERSEPHONE rises to her feet, and amidst a contrivance of confused darkness HADES is seen rushing
from behind. He seizes her and drags her backward. Her basket is thrown up and the flowers scattered.]

ACT II

CHORUS
Bright day succeedeth unto day—
Night to pensive night—
With his towering ray
Of all-fathering light—
With the solemn trance
Of her starry dance.—

Nought is new or strange
In the eternal change.—

As the light clouds fly
O'er the tree-tops high,
So the days go by.—

Ripples that arrive
On the sunny shore,
Dying to their live
Music evermore.—

Like pearls on a thread,—
Like notes of a song,—
Like the measur'd tread
Of a dancing throng.—

Ocëanides are we,
Nereids of the foam,
But we left the sea
On the earth to roam
With the fairest Queen
That the world hath seen.—
Why amidst our play
Was she sped away?—

Over hill and plain
We have sought in vain;
She comes not again.—

Not the Naiads knew
On their dewy lawns:—
Not the laughing crew
Of the leaping Fauns.—

Now, since she is gone,
All our dance is slow,
All our joy is done,
And our song is woe.—

Saw ye the mighty Mother, where she went
Searching the land?
Nor night nor day resting from her lament,
With smoky torch in hand.
Her godhead in the passion of a sorrow spent
Which not her mind coud suffer, nor heart withstand?—

Enlanguor'd like a fasting lioness,
That prowls around
Robb'd of her whelps, in fury comfortless
Until her lost be found:
Implacable and terrible in her wild distress;
And thro' the affrighted country her roars resound.—

3

But lo! what form is there? Thine eyes awaken!
See! see! O say,
Is not that she, the furious, the forsaken?
She cometh, lo! this way;
Her golden-rippling hair upon her shoulders shaken,
And all her visage troubled with deep dismay.

DEMETER (entering)
Here is the hateful spot, the hollow rock
Whence the fierce ravisher sprang forth—
(seeing the nymphs) Ah! Ye!
I know you well: ye are the nymphs of Ocean.
Ye, graceful as your watery names
And idle as the mimic flames
That skip upon his briny floor,
When the hot sun smiteth thereo'er;
Why did ye leave your native waves?
Did false Poseidon, to my hurt
Leagued with my foe, bid you desert
Your opalescent pearly caves,
Your dances on the shelly strand?

CHORUS
Poseidon gave us no command,
Lady; it was thy child Persephone,
Whose beauty drew us from the sea.

DEMETER
Ill company ye lent, ill-fated guards!
How was she stolen from your distracted eyes?

CHORUS
There, where thou standest now, stood she companion'd
By wise Athena and bright Artemis.
We in flower-gathering dance and idle song
Were wander'd off apart; we fear'd no wrong.

DEMETER

In heav'n I heard her cry: ye nothing heard?

CHORUS

We heard no cry—How coudst thou hear in heaven?
Ask us not óf her:—we have nought to tell.—

DEMETER

I seek not knowledge óf you, for I know.

CHORUS

Thou knowest? Ah, mighty Queen, deign then to tell
If thou hast found HERMES Tell us—tell us—tell!

DEMETER

Oh, there are calls that love can hear,
That strike not on the outward ear.
None heard save I: but with a dart
Of lightning-pain it pierc'd my heart,
That call for aid, that cry of fear.
It echo'd from the mountain-steeps
Down to the dark of Ocean-deeps;
O'er all the isle, from ev'ry hill
It pierc'd my heart and echoes still,
Ay me! Ay me!

CHORUS

Where is she, O mighty Queen?—Tell us—O tell!—

DEMETER

Swift unto earth, in frenzy led
By Cora's cry, from heav'n I sped.
Immortal terror froze my mind:
I fear'd, ev'n as I yearn'd to find
My child, my joy, faln from my care
Wrong'd or distresst, I knew not where,
Cora, my Cora!
Nor thought I whither first to fly,
Answ'ring the appeal of that wild cry:
But still it drew me till I came
To Enna, calling still her name,
Cora, my Cora!

CHORUS

If thou hast found her, tell us, Queen, O tell!

DEMETER

Nine days I wander'd o'er the land.
From Enna to the eastern strand

I sought, and when the first night came
I lit my torch in Etna's flame.
But neither 'mid the chestnut woods
That rustle o'er his stony floods;
Nor yet at daybreak on the meads
Where bountiful Symaethus leads
His chaunting boatmen to the main;
Nor where the road on Hybla's plain
Is skirted by the spacious corn;
Nor where embattled Syracuse
With lustrous temple fronts the morn;
Nor yet by dolphin'd Arethuse;
Nor when I crossed Anapus wide,
Where Cyane, his reedy bride,
Uprushing from her crystal well,
Doth not his cold embrace repel;
Nor yet by western Eryx, where
Gay Aphrodite high in air
Beams gladness from her marble chair;
Nor 'mong the mountains that enfold
Panormos in her shell of gold,
Found I my Cora: no reply
Came to my call, my helpless cry,
Cora, my Cora!

CHORUS
Hast thou not found her, then? Tell us—O tell!

DEMETER
What wonder that I never found
Her whom I sought on mortal ground,
When she—(now will ye understand?)—
Dwelt in the land that is no land,
The fruitless and unseason'd plain
Where all lost things are found again;
Where man's distract imaginings
Head-downward hang on bat-like wings,
'Mid mummied hopes, sleep-walking cares,
Crest-faln illusions and despairs,
The tortur'd memories of crime,
The outcasts of forgotten time?

CHORUS
Where is she, Queen?—where?—where?

DEMETER
Nor had I known,
Had not himself high Helios seen and told me.

CHORUS
Alas! Alas! We cannot understand—
We pray, dear Queen, may great Zeus comfort thee.

DEMETER
Yea, pray to Zeus; but pray ye for yourselves,
That he have pity on you, for there is need.
Or let Zeus hear a strange, unwonted prayer
That in his peril he will aid himself;
For I have said, nor coud his Stygian oath
Add any sanction to a mother's word,
That, if he give not back my daughter to me,
Him will I slay, and lock his pining ghost
In sleepy prisons of unhallowing hell.

CHORUS (aside)
Alas! alas! she is distraught with grief.—
What comfort can we make?— How reason with her?—
(to DEMETER) This coud not be, great Queen. How coud it be
That Zeus should be destroy'd, or thou destroy him?

DEMETER
Yea, and you too: so make your prayer betimes.

CHORUS
We pray thee, Lady, sit thou on this bank
And we will bring thee food; or if thou thirst,
Water. We know too in what cooling caves
The sly Fauns have bestow'd their skins of wine.

DEMETER
Ye simple creatures, I need not these things,
And stand above your pity. Think ye me
A woman of the earth derang'd with grief?
Nay, nay: but I have pity on your pity,
And for your kindness I will ease the trouble
Wherewith it wounds your gentleness: attend!
Ye see this jewel here, that from my neck
Hangs by this golden chain.

[They crowd near to see.

Look, 'tis a picture,
'Tis of Persephone.

CHORUS
How?—Is that she?—

A crown she weareth.—She was never wont
Thus ...—nor her robe thus—and her countenance
Hath not the smile which drew us from the sea.

DEMETER
Daedalus cut it, in the year he made
The Zibian Aphrodite, and Hephaestus
O'erlookt and praised the work. I treasure it
Beyond all other jewels that I have,
And on this chain I guard it. Say now: think ye
It cannot fall loose until every link
Of all the chain be broken, or if one
Break, will it fall?

CHORUS
Surely if one break, Lady,
The chain is broken and the jewel falls.

'Tis so. Now hearken diligently. All life
Is as this chain, and Zeus is as the jewel.
The universal life dwells first in the Earth,
The stones and soil; therefrom the plants and trees
Exhale their being; and on them the brutes
Feeding elaborate their sentient life,
And from these twain mankind; and in mankind
A spirit lastly is form'd of subtler sort
Whereon the high gods live, sustain'd thereby,
And feeding on it, as plants on the soil,
Or animals on plants. Now see! I hold,
As well ye know, one whole link of this chain:
If I should kill the plants, must not man perish?
And if he perish, then the gods must die.

CHORUS
If this were so, thou wouldst destroy thyself.

DEMETER
And therefore Zeus will not believe my word.

CHORUS
Nor we believe thee, Lady: it cannot be
That thou shouldst seek to mend a private fortune
By universal ruin, and restore
Thy daughter by destruction of thyself.

DEMETER
Ye are not mothers, or ye would not wonder.
In me, who hold from great all-mother Rhea

Heritage of essential motherhood,
Ye would look rather for unbounded passion.
Coud I, the tenderness of Nature's heart,
Exist, were I unheedful to protect
From wrong and ill the being that I gave,
The unweeting passions that I fondly nurtured
To hopes of glory, the young confidence
In growing happiness? Shall I throw by
As self-delusion the supreme ambition,
Which I encourag'd till parental fondness
Bore the prophetic blessing, on whose truth
My spirit throve? Oh never! nay, nay, nay!
That were the one disaster, and if aid
I cannot, I can mightily avenge.
On irremediable wrong I shrink not
To pile immortal ruin, there to lie
As trophies on a carven tomb: nor less
For that no memory of my deed survive,
Nor any eye to see, nor tongue to tell.

CHORUS
So vast injustice, Lady, were not good.

DEMETER
To you I seem unjust involving man.

CHORUS
Why should man suffer in thy feud with Zeus?

DEMETER
Let Zeus relent. There is no other way.
I will destroy the seeds of plant and tree:
Vineyard and orchard, oliveyard and cornland
Shall all withhold their fruits, and in their stead
Shall flourish the gay blooms that Cora loved.
There shall be dearth, and yet so gay the dearth
That all the land shall look in holiday
With mockery of foison; every field
With splendour aflame. For wheat the useless poppy
In sheeted scarlet; and for barley and oats
The blue and yellow weeds that mock men's toil,
Centaury and marigold in chequer'd plots:
Where seed is sown, or none, shall dandelions
And wretched ragwort vie, orchis and iris
And garish daisy, and for every flower
That in this vale she pluckt, shall spring a thousand.
Where'er she slept anemones shall crowd,
And the sweet violet. These things shall ye see.

—But I behold him whom I came to meet,
Hermes:—he, be he laden howsoe'er,
Will heavier laden to his lord return.

HERMES (entering).
Mighty Demeter, Mother of the seasons,
Bountiful all-sustainer, fairest daughter
Of arch-ancestral Rhea,—to thee Zeus sendeth
Kindly message. He grieves seeing thy godhead
Offended wrongly at eternal justice,
'Gainst destiny ordain'd idly revolting.
Ever will he, thy brother, honour thee
And willingly aid thee: but since now thy daughter
Is raised to a place on the tripartite throne,
He finds thee honour'd duly and not injur'd.
Wherefore he bids thee now lament no more,
But with thy presence grace the courts of heav'n.

DEMETER
Bright Hermes, Argus-slayer, born of Maia,
Who bearest empty words, the mask of war,
To Zeus make thine own words, that thou hast found me
Offended,—that I still lament my daughter,
Nor heed his summons to the courts of heav'n.

HERMES
Giv'st thou me nought but these relentless words?

DEMETER
I send not words, nor dost thou carry deeds.
But know, since heav'n denies my claim, I take
Earth for my battle-field. Curse and defiance
Shall shake his throne, and, readier then for justice,
Zeus will enquire my terms: thou, on that day,
Remember them; that he shall bid thee lead
Persephone from Hades by the hand,
And on this spot, whence she was stol'n, restore her
Into mine arms. Execute that; and praise
Shall rise from earth and peace return to heav'n.

HERMES
How dare I carry unto Zeus thy threats?

DEMETER
Approach him with a gift: this little wallet.

[Giving a little bag of seeds.

I will not see thee again until the day
Thou lead my daughter hither thro' the gates of Hell.

[Going.

HERMES
Ah! mighty Queen, the lightness of thy gift
Is greater burden than thy weighty words.

[Exeunt severally r. and l.

CHORUS
(1) Sisters! what have we heard!
Our fair Persephone, the flower of the earth,
By Hades stolen away, his queen to be.
(others) Alas!—alas!—ay me!
(2) And great Demeter's bold relentless word
To Hermes given,
Threatening mankind with dearth.
(others) Ay me! alas! alas!—
(3 or 1) She in her sorrow strong
Fears not to impeach the King of Heaven,
And combat wrong with wrong.—
(others confusedly) What can we do?—Alas!—
Back to our ocean-haunts return
To weep and mourn.—
What use to mourn?—
Nay, nay!—Away with sorrow:
Let us forget to-day
And look for joy to-morrow:—
[(1) Nay, nay! hearken to me!]
Nay, how forget that on us too,—
Yea, on us all
The curse will fall.—
[(1) Hearken! I say!]
What can we do? Alas! alas!
(1) Hearken! There's nought so light,
Nothing of weight so small,
But that in even balance 'twill avail
Wholly to turn the scale.
Let us our feeble force unite,
And giving voice to tears,
Assail Poseidon's ears;
Rob pleasure from his days,
Darken with sorrow all his ways,
Until his shifty mind
Become to pity inclined,
And 'gainst his brother turn.

(others) 'Tis well, thou sayest well.
(2) Yea; for if Zeus should learn
That earth and sea were both combined
Against his cruel intent,
Sooner will he relent.
(others) 'Tis well—we do it—'tis well.—
(1) Come let us vow. Vow all with one accord
To harden every heart
Till we have won Poseidon to our part.
(all) We vow—we do it—we vow.
(1) Till we have conquer'd heav'n's almighty lord
And seen Persephone restored.
(all) We vow—we vow.
(1) Come then all; and, as ye go,
Begin the song of woe.

SONG

Close up, bright flow'rs, and hang the head,
Ye beauties of the plain,
The Queen of Spring is with the dead,
Ye deck the earth in vain.
From your deserted vale we fly,
And where the salt waves mourn
Our song shall swell their burd'ning sigh
Until sweet joy return.

ACT III

CHORUS

SONG

Lo where the virgin veilëd in airy beams,
All-holy Morn, in splendor awakening,
Heav'n's gate hath unbarrèd, the golden
Aerial lattices set open.

With music endeth night's prisoning terror,
With flow'ry incense: Haste to salute the sun,
That for the day's chase, like a huntsman,
With flashing arms cometh o'er the mountain.

Inter se. That were a song for Artemis—I have heard
Men thus salute the rising sun in spring—
—See, we have wreaths enough and garlands plenty

To hide our lov'd Persephone from sight
If she should come.—But think you she will come?—
If one might trust the heavens, it is a morn
Promising happiness—'Tis like the day
That brought us all our grief a year ago.—

ODE
O that the earth, or only this fair isle wer' ours
Amid the ocean's blue billows,
With flow'ry woodland, stately mountain and valley,
Cascading and lilied river;
Nor ever a mortal envious, laborious,
By anguish or dull care opprest,
Should come polluting with remorseful countenance
Our haunt of easy gaiety.
For us the grassy slopes, the country's airiness,
The lofty whispering forest,
Where rapturously Philomel invoketh the night
And million eager throats the morn;
With doves at evening softly cooing, and mellow
Cadences of the dewy thrush.
We love the gentle deer, the nimble antelope;
Mice love we and springing squirrels;
To watch the gaudy flies visit the blooms, to hear
On ev'ry mead the grasshopper.
All thro' the spring-tide, thro' the indolent summer,
(If only this fair isle wer' ours)
Here might we dwell, forgetful of the weedy caves
Beneath the ocean's blue billows.

Enter DEMETER.

CHORUS
Hail, mighty Mother!—Welcome, great Demeter!—
(1) This day bring joy to thee, and peace to man!

DEMETER
I welcome you, my loving true allies,
And thank you, who for me your gentle tempers
Have stiffen'd in rebellion, and so long
Harass'd the foe. Here on this field of flowers
I have bid you share my victory or defeat.
For Hermes hath this day command from Zeus
To lead our lost Persephone from Hell,
Hither whence she was stolen.—And yet, alas!
Tho' Zeus is won, some secret power thwarts me;
All is not won: a cloud is o'er my spirit.

Wherefore not yet I boast, nor will rejoice
Till mine eyes see her, and my arms enfold her,
And breast to breast we meet in fond embrace.

CHORUS
Well hast thou fought, great goddess, so to wrest
Zeus from his word. We thank thee, call'd to share
Thy triumph, and rejoice. Yet O, we pray,
Make thou this day a day of peace for man!
Even if Persephone be not restored,
Whether Aidoneus hold her or release,
Relent thou.—Stay thine anger, mighty goddess;
Nor with thy hateful famine slay mankind.

DEMETER
Say not that word 'relent' lest Hades hear!

CHORUS
Consider rather if mankind should hear.

DEMETER
Do ye love man?

CHORUS
We have seen his sorrows, Lady ...

DEMETER
And what can ye have seen that I know not?—
His sorrow?—Ah my sorrow!—and ye bid
Me to relent; whose deeds of fond compassion
Have in this year of agony built up
A story for all time that shall go wand'ring
Further than I have wander'd;—whereto all ears
Shall hearken ever, as ye will hearken now.

CHORUS
Happy are we, who first shall hear the tale
From thine own lips, and tell it to the sea.

DEMETER
Attend then while I tell.—
—Parting from Hermes hence, anger'd at heart,
Self-exiled from the heav'ns, forgone, alone,
My anguish fasten'd on me, as I went
Wandering an alien in the haunts of men.
To screen my woe I put my godhead off,
Taking the likeness of a worthy dame,
A woman of the people well in years;

Till going unobserv'd, it irked me soon
To be unoccupy'd save by my grief,
While men might find distraction for their sorrows
In useful toil. Then, of my pity rather
Than hope to find their simple cure my own,
I took resolve to share and serve their needs,
And be as one of them.

CHORUS
Ah, mighty goddess,
Coudst thou so put thy dignities away,
And suffer the familiar brunt of men?

DEMETER
In all things even as they.—And sitting down
One evening at Eleusis, by the well
Under an olive-tree, likening myself
Outwardly to some kindly-hearted matron,
Whose wisdom and experience are of worth
Either where childhood clamorously speaks
The engrossing charge of Aphrodite's gifts,
Or merry maidens in wide-echoing halls
Want sober governance;—to me, as there
I sat, the daughters of King Keleos came,
Tall noble damsels, as kings' daughters are,
And, marking me a stranger, they drew from me
A tale told so engagingly, that they
Grew fain to find employment for my skill;
—As men devise in mutual recompense,
Hoping the main advantage for themselves;—
And so they bad me follow, and I enter'd
The palace of King Keleos, and received
There on my knees the youngest of the house,
A babe, to nurse him as a mother would:
And in that menial service I was proud
To outrun duty and trust: and there I liv'd
Disguised among the maidens many months.

CHORUS
Often as have our guesses aim'd, dear Lady,
Where thou didst hide thyself, oft as we wonder'd
What chosen work was thine, none ever thought
That thou didst deign to tend a mortal babe.

DEMETER
What life I led shall be for men to tell.
But for this babe, the nursling of my sorrow,
Whose peevish cry was my consoling care,

How much I came to love him ye shall hear.

CHORUS
What was he named, Lady?

DEMETER
Demophoön.
Yea, ye shall hear how much I came to love him.
For in his small epitome I read
The trouble of mankind; in him I saw
The hero's helplessness, the countless perils
In ambush of life's promise, the desire
Blind and instinctive, and the will perverse.
His petty needs were man's necessities;
In him I nurst all mortal natur', embrac'd
With whole affection to my breast, and lull'd
Wailing humanity upon my knee.

CHORUS
We see thou wilt not now destroy mankind.

DEMETER
What I coud do to save man was my thought.
And, since my love was center'd in the boy,
My thought was first for him, to rescue him;
That, thro' my providence, he ne'er should know
Suffering, nor disease, nor fear of death
Therefore I fed him on immortal food,
And should have gain'd my wish, so well he throve,
But by ill-chance it hapt, once, as I held him
Bathed in the fire at midnight (as was my wont),—
His mother stole upon us, and ascare
At the strange sight, screaming in loud dismay
Compel'd me to unmask, and leave for ever
The halls of Keleos, and my work undone.

CHORUS
'Twas pity that she came!—Didst thou not grieve to lose
The small Demophoön?—Coudst thou not save him?

DEMETER
I had been blinded. Think ye for yourselves ...
What vantage were it to mankind at large
That one should be immortal,—if all beside
Must die and suffer misery as before?

CHORUS
Nay, truly. And great envy borne to one

So favour'd might have more embitter'd all.

DEMETER
I had been foolish. My sojourn with men
Had warpt my mind with mortal tenderness.
So, questioning myself what real gift
I might bestow on man to help his state,
I saw that sorrow was his life-companion,
To be embrac't bravely, not weakly shun'd:
That as by toil man winneth happiness,
Thro' tribulation he must come to peace.
How to make sorrow his friend then,—this my task.
Here was a mystery ... and how persuade
This thorny truth?... Ye do not hearken me.

CHORUS
Yea, honour'd goddess, yea, we hearken still:
Stint not thy tale.

DEMETER
Ye might not understand.
My tale to you must be a tale of deeds—
How first I bade King Keleos build for me
A temple in Eleusis, and ordain'd
My worship, and the mysteries of my thought;
Where in the sorrow that I underwent
Man's state is pattern'd; and in picture shewn
The way of his salvation.... Now with me
—Here is a matter grateful to your ears—
Your lov'd Persephone hath equal honour,
And in the spring her festival of flowers:
And if she should return ...

[Listening.

Ah! hark! what hear I?

CHORUS
We hear no sound.

DEMETER
Hush ye! Hermes: he comes.

CHORUS
What hearest thou?

DEMETER
Hermes; and not alone.

She is there. 'Tis she: I have won.

CHORUS
Where? where?

DEMETER (aside)
Ah! can it be that out of sorrow's night,
From tears, from yearning pain, from long despair,
Into joy's sunlight I shall come again?—
Aside! stand ye aside!

Enter HERMES leading PERSEPHONE.

HERMES
Mighty Demeter, lo! I execute
The will of Zeus and here restore thy daughter.

DEMETER
I have won.

PERSEPHONE
Sweet Mother, thy embrace is as the welcome
Of all the earth, thy kiss the breath of life.

DEMETER
Ah! but to me, Cora! Thy voice again...
My tongue is trammel'd with excess of joy.

PERSEPHONE
Arise, my nymphs, my Oceanides!
My Nereids all, arise! and welcome me!
Put off your strange solemnity! arise!

CHORUS
Welcome! all welcome, fair Persephone!
(1) We came to welcome thee, but fell abash'd
Seeing thy purple robe and crystal crown.

PERSEPHONE
Arise and serve my pleasure as of yore.

DEMETER
And thou too doff thy strange solemnity,
That all may see thee as thou art, my Cora,
Restor'd and ever mine. Put off thy crown!

PERSEPHONE
Awhile! dear Mother—what thou say'st is true;

I am restor'd to thee, and evermore
Shall be restor'd. Yet am I none the less
Evermore Queen of Hades: and 'tis meet
I wear the crown, the symbol of my reign.

DEMETER
What words are these, my Cora! Evermore
Restor'd to me thou say'st ... 'tis well—but then
Evermore Queen of Hades ... what is this?
I had a dark foreboding till I saw thee:
Alas, alas! it lives again: destroy it!
Solve me this riddle quickly, if thou mayest.

PERSEPHONE
Let Hermes speak, nor fear thou. All is well.

HERMES
Divine Demeter, thou hast won thy will,
And the command of Zeus have I obey'd.
Thy daughter is restor'd, and evermore
Shall be restor'd to thee as on this day.
But Hades holding to his bride, the Fates
Were kind also to him, that she should be
His queen in Hades as thy child on earth.
Yearly, as spring-tide cometh, she is thine
While flowers bloom and all the land is gay;
But when thy corn is gather'd, and the fields
Are bare, and earth withdraws her budding life
From the sharp bite of winter's angry fang,
Yearly will she return and hold her throne
With great Aidoneus and the living dead:
And she hath eaten with him of such fruit
As holds her his true bride for evermore.

DEMETER
Alas! alas!

PERSEPHONE
Rejoice, dear Mother Let not vain lament
Trouble our joy this day, nor idle tears.

DEMETER
Alas! from my own deed my trouble comes:
He gave thee of the fruit which I had curs'd:
I made the poison that enchanted thee.

PERSEPHONE
Repent not in thy triumph, but rejoice,

Who hast thy will in all, as I have mine.

DEMETER
I have but half my will, how hast thou more?

PERSEPHONE
It was my childish fancy (thou rememb'rest),
I would be goddess of the flowers: I thought
That men should innocently honour me
With bloodless sacrifice and spring-tide joy.
Now Fate, that look'd contrary, hath fulfill'd
My project with mysterious efficacy:
And as a plant that yearly dieth down
When summer is o'er, and hideth in the earth,
Nor showeth promise in its wither'd leaves
That it shall reawaken and put forth
Its blossoms any more to deck the spring;
So I, the mutual symbol of my choice,
Shall die with winter, and with spring revive.
How without winter coud I have my spring?
How come to resurrection without death?
Lo thus our joyful meeting of to-day,
Born of our separation, shall renew
Its annual ecstasy, by grief refresht:
And no more pall than doth the joy of spring
Yearly returning to the hearts of men.
See then the accomplishment of all my hope:
Rejoice, and think not to put off my crown.

DEMETER
What hast thou seen below to reconcile thee
To the dark moiety of thy strange fate?

PERSEPHONE
Where have I been, mother? what have I seen?
The downward pathway to the gates of death:
The skeleton of earthly being, stript
Of all disguise: the sudden void of night:
The spectral records of unwholesome fear:—
Why was it given to me to see these things?
The ruin'd godheads, disesteem'd, condemn'd
To toil of deathless mockery: conquerors
In the reverse of glory, doom'd to rule
The multitudinous army of their crimes:
The naked retribution of all wrong:—
Why was it given to me to see such things?

DEMETER

Not without terror, as I think, thou speakest,
Nor as one reconcil'd to brook return.

PERSEPHONE
But since I have seen these things, with salt and fire
My spirit is purged, and by this crystal crown
Terror is tamed within me. If my words
Seem'd to be tinged with terror, 'twas because
I knew one hour of terror (on the day
That took me hence) and with that memory
Colour'd my speech, using the terms which paint
The blindfold fears of men, who little reckon
How they by holy innocence and love,
By reverence and gentle lives may win
A title to the fair Elysian fields,
Where the good spirits dwell in ease and light
And entertainment of those fair desires
That made earth beautiful ... brave souls that spent
Their lives for liberty and truth, grave seers
Whose vision conquer'd darkness, pious poets
Whose words have won Apollo's deathless praise,
Who all escape Hell's mysteries, nor come nigh
The Cave of Cacophysia.

DEMETER
Mysteries!
What mysteries are these? and what the Cave?

PERSEPHONE
The mysteries of evil, and the cave
Of blackness that obscures them. Even in hell
The worst is hidden, and unfructuous night
Stifles her essence in her truthless heart.

DEMETER
What is the arch-falsity? I seek to know
The mystery of evil. Hast thou seen it?

PERSEPHONE
I have seen it. Coud I truly rule my kingdom
Not having seen it?

DEMETER
Tell me what it is.

PERSEPHONE
'Tis not that I forget it; tho' the thought
Is banisht from me. But 'tis like a dream

Whose sense is an impression lacking words.

DEMETER
If it would pain thee telling ...

PERSEPHONE
Nay, but surely
The words of gods and men are names of things
And thoughts accustom'd: but of things unknown
And unimagin'd are no words at all.

DEMETER
And yet will words sometimes outrun the thought.

PERSEPHONE
What can be spoken is nothing: 'twere a path
That leading t'ward some prospect ne'er arrived.

DEMETER
The more thou holdest back, the more I long.

PERSEPHONE
The outward aspect only mocks my words.

DEMETER
Yet what is outward easy is to tell.

PERSEPHONE
Something is possible. This cavern lies
In very midmost of deep-hollow'd hell.
O'er its torn mouth the black Plutonic rock
Is split in sharp disorder'd pinnacles
And broken ledges, whereon sit, like apes
Upon a wither'd tree, the hideous sins
Of all the world: once having seen within
The magnetism is heavy on them, and they crawl
Palsied with filthy thought upon the peaks;
Or, squatting thro' long ages, have become
Rooted like plants into the griping clefts:
And there they pullulate, and moan, and strew
The rock with fragments of their mildew'd growth.

DEMETER
Cora, my child! and hast thou seen these things!

PERSEPHONE
Nay but the outward aspect, figur'd thus
In mere material loathsomeness, is nought

Beside the mystery that is hid within.

DEMETER
Search thou for words, I pray, somewhat to tell.

PERSEPHONE
Are there not matters past the thought of men
Or gods to know?

DEMETER
Thou meanest wherefore things
Should be at all? Or, if they be, why thus,
As hot, cold, hard and soft: and wherefore Zeus
Had but two brothers; why the stars of heaven
Are so innumerable, constellated
Just as they are; or why this Sicily
Should be three-corner'd? Yes, thou sayest well,
Why things are as they are, nor gods nor men
Can know. We say that Fate appointed thus,
And are content.—

PERSEPHONE
Suppose, dear Mother, there wer' a temple in heaven,
Which, dedicated to the unknown Cause
And worship of the unseen, had power to draw
All that was worthy and good within its gate:
And that the spirits who enter'd there became
Not only purified and comforted,
But that the mysteries of the shrine were such,
That the initiated bathed in light
Of infinite intelligence, and saw
The meaning and the reason of all things,
All at a glance distinctly, and perceived
The origin of all things to be good,
And the énd good, and that what appears as evil
Is as a film of dust, that faln thereon,
May,—at one stroke of the hand,—
Be brush'd away, and show the good beneath,
Solid and fair and shining: If moreover
This blessëd vision were of so great power
That none coud e'er forget it or relapse
To doubtful ignorance:—I say, dear Mother,
Suppose that there were such a temple in heaven.

DEMETER
O child, my child! that were a temple indeed.
'Tis such a temple as man needs on earth;
A holy shrine that makes no pact with sin,

A worthy shrine to draw the worthy and good,
A shrine of wisdom trifling not with folly,
A shrine of beauty, where the initiated
Drank love and light.... Strange thou shouldst speak of it.
I have inaugurated such a temple
These last days in Eleusis, have ordain'd
These very mysteries!—Strange thou speakest of it.
But by what path return we to the Cave
Of Cacophysia?

PERSEPHONE
By this path, dear Mother.
The Cave of Cacophysia is in all things
T'ward evil, as that temple were t'ward good.
I enter'd in. Outside the darkness was
But as accumulated sunlessness;
Within 'twas positive as light itself,
A blackness that extinguished: Yet I knew,
For Hades told me, that I was to see;
And so I waited, till a forking flash
Of sudden lightning dazzlingly reveal'd
All at a glance. As on a pitchy night
The warder of some high acropolis
Looks down into the dark, and suddenly
Sees all the city with its roofs and streets,
Houses and walls, clear as in summer noon,
And ere he think of it, 'tis dark again,—
So I saw all within the Cave, and held
The vision, 'twas so burnt upon my sense.

DEMETER
What saw'st thou, child? what saw'st thou?

PERSEPHONE
Nay, the things
Not to be told, because there are no words
Of gods or men to paint the inscrutable
And full initiation of hell.—I saw
The meaning and the reason of all things,
All at a glance, and in that glance perceiv'd
The origin of all things to be evil,
And the énd evil: that what seems as good
Is as a bloom of gold that spread thereo'er
May, by one stroke of the hand,
Be brush'd away, and leave the ill beneath
Solid and foul and black....

DEMETER

Now tell me, child,
If Hades love thee, that he sent thee thither.

PERSEPHONE
He said it coud not harm me: and I think
It hath not.

[Going up to DEMETETER, who kisses her.

DEMETER
Nay it hath not, ... and I know
The power of evil is no power at all
Against eternal good. 'Tis fire on water,
As darkness against sunlight, like a dream
To waken'd will. Foolish was I to fear
That aught coud hurt thee, Cora. But to-day
Speak we no more.... This mystery of Hell
Will do me service: I'll not tell thee now:
But sure it is that Fate o'erruleth all
For good or ill: and we (no more than men)
Have power to oppose, nor any will nor choice
Beyond such wisdom as a fisher hath
Who driven by sudden gale far out to sea
Handles his fragile boat safe thro' the waves,
Making what harbour the wild storm allows.
To-day hard-featured and inscrutable Fate
Stands to mine eyes reveal'd, nor frowns upon me.
I thought to find thee as I knew thee, and fear'd
Only to find thee sorrowful: I find thee
Far other than thou wert, nor hurt by Hell.
I thought I must console thee, but 'tis thou
Playest the comforter: I thought to teach thee,
And had prepared my lesson, word by word;
But thou art still beyond me. One thing only
Of all my predetermin'd plan endures:
My purpose was to bid thee to Eleusis
For thy spring festival, which three days hence
Inaugurates my temple. Thou wilt come?

PERSEPHONE
I come. And art thou reconcil'd, dear Mother?

DEMETER
Joy and surprise make tempest in my mind;
When their bright stir is o'er, there will be peace.
But ere we leave this flowery field, the scene
Of strange and beauteous memories evermore,
I thank thee, Hermes, for thy willing service.

PERSEPHONE
I thank thee, son of Maia, and bid farewell.

HERMES
Have thy joy now, great Mother; and have thou joy,
Fairest Persephone, Queen of the Spring.

CHORUS
Fair Persephone, garlands we bring thee,
Flow'rs and spring-tide welcome sing thee.
Hades held thee not,
Darkness quell'd thee not.
Gay and joyful welcome!
Welcome, Queen, evermore.
Earth shall own thee,
Thy nymphs crown thee,
Garland thee and crown thee,
Crown thee Queen evermore.

Robert Seymour Bridges – A Short Biography

Robert Seymour Bridges, OM was born on 23 October 1844 at Walmer in Kent where he spent his early childhood in a house overlooking the anchoring ground of the British fleet. He was the fourth son and eighth child of John Thomas Bridges (1805–1853) and Harriett Elizabeth Affleck (1807–1897).

His father died at the age of only 47 in 1853 and a year later his mother remarried and the family relocated to Rochdale, where his stepfather, John Edward Nassau Molesworth, was the vicar.

In 1854 Bridges was sent to the elite public school of Eton College and attended there until 1863. Whilst there he met the poet Digby Mackworth Dolben and Lionel Muirhead, who became a lifelong friend.

After Eton he went to Oxford and the Corpus Christi College. Whilst studying he became good friends with Gerald Manley Hopkins. Hopkins is now considered the superior poet and Bridges probably knew this or at least was a great admirer as he was essential in ensuring the publication of the complete works of Hopkins in 1918. His edition of Hopkins's poems is considered a major contribution to English literature.

He received his degree and graduated from Oxford in 1867 with a second class in literae humaniores. His initial thought was to enter religious life with the Church of England and he travelled to the Middle East in furtherance of his knowledge on the subject. But instead he decided that life as a physician would be a better path and after learning German for eight months in Germany (that being the language of many scientific papers at the time) he began his study of medicine at St. Bartholomew's Hospital in 1869. His long term hope was that by the age of forty he could retire from medicine to devote himself to writing.

Bridges failed his final medical examinations in 1873 and as unable to immediately retake the papers, spent six months in Italy learning Italian and as much as he could about Italian art. In July 1874 he went to study medicine in Dublin. Re-examined in December of that year, he obtained his MB and became a house physician to Dr Patrick Black at St Bartholomew's Hospital.

He practiced as a casualty physician at this teaching hospital where he also engaged in a series of highly critical remarks about the Victorian medical establishment. Such was his workload that he claimed that whilst working as a young doctor he saw a staggering 30,940 patients in one year.

After being a house physician at St Bartholomew's he later became casualty physician and later assistant physician at the Hospital for Sick Children, Great Ormond Street, and then physician at Great Northern Hospital, Holloway.

A bout of severe pneumonia and lung disease forced his retirement from the medical profession in 1882 and so slightly ahead of schedule he began his literary career in earnest.

However he had, prior to this, been writing for several years. His first collection of poems having been published in 1873. Indeed its worth pointing out that his early materials were published privately, mainly to be given away to friends and his small circle of admirers as they sold little. It took Bridges some time to gain traction and a wider audience.

After his illness and a trip to Italy with Muirhead, Bridges moved with his mother to Yattendon in Berkshire.

It was during his residence in Yattendon, from 1882 to 1904, that Bridges wrote most of his best-known lyrics as well as eight plays and two masques, all in verse.

It was here that he first met and then in 1884 he married Monica Waterhouse, daughter of Alfred Waterhouse R.A., the famous architect. The couple had three children: Elizabeth (1887–1977), Margaret (1889–1926), and Edward Ettingdene Bridges (1892–1969). They would spend the rest of their lives in rural seclusion, in an idyllic marriage, first at Yattendon, Berkshire, then later at Boars Hill, Oxford

Bridges made an important contribution to hymnody with the publication in 1899 of his Yattendon Hymnal, which he created specifically for musical reasons. This collection of hymns, although not a financial success, became a bridge between the Victorian hymnody of the last half of the 19th century and the modern hymnody of the early 20th century. He was a chorister at Yattendon church for 18 years.

In 1902 Monica and his daughter Margaret became seriously ill with tuberculosis, and a move from Yattendon to a healthier climate was in order.

After living in several temporary homes they moved abroad to spend a year in Switzerland, and finally returning settled again in England at Chilswell House, which Bridges had designed and which was built on Boar's Hill overlooking Oxford University.

Bridges was elected to the Fellowship of the Royal College of Physicians of London in 1900.

His greatest achievement though was still some years ahead of him. The office of Poet Laureate was held by Alfred Austin but with his death it was offered first to Rudyard Kipling, who refused it, and thence to Bridges. He was appointed Poet Laureate in 1913 by George V, the only medical graduate to have ever held the office. It seems a strange choice given the 'write to order' brief of Poet Laureate but Bridges accepted and must have known of the strictures.

That same year along with Henry Bradley and Walter Raleigh he founded the Society for Pure English.

Bridges received advice from the young phonetician David Abercrombie on the reformed spelling system he was devising for the publication of his collected essays (later published in seven volumes by Oxford University Press, with the help of the distinguished typographer Stanley Morison, who designed the new letters). Thus Robert Bridges contributed to phonetics.

The office of Poet Laureate has been held by many great and well known poets such as John Dryden, William Wordsworth and Alfred Lord Tennyson.

Bridges at this stage was not highly regarded nor well known but more a safe pair of hands in a World rapidly being overshadowed by the storms about to erupt over Europe and the First World War.

The events of the First World War, including the wounding of his son, Edward, had a sobering effect on Bridges' poetry. He composed fiercely patriotic poems and letters, and in 1915 edited a volume of prose and poetry, The Spirit of Man, intended to appeal to readers living in war times.

One area where his work did resonate though was with a great many composers and specifically British. Many set his poetry to music and among them were Hubert Parry, Gustav Holst and Gerald Finzi.

Despite being made poet laureate Bridges was never a very well-known poet and only achieved his great popularity shortly before his death with The Testament of Beauty.

His best-known poems are found in the two earlier volumes of Shorter Poems (1890, 1894). His talents did not stop at poetry and his works include verse plays and literary criticism, including a study of the work of fellow poet John Keats.

As a poet Bridges stands rather apart from the tide of modern English verse, but his work has had great influence in a select circle, by its restraint, purity, precision, and delicacy yet strength of expression. It embodies a distinct theory of prosody. Bridges' deep faith underpinned much of his work.

In the book Milton's Prosody, he took an empirical approach to examining Milton's use of blank verse, and developed the somewhat controversial theory that Milton's practice was essentially syllabic. He considered free verse to be too limiting, and explained his position in the essay "Humdrum and Harum-Scarum".

Bridge's own efforts to "free" verse resulted in the poems he called "Neo-Miltonic Syllabics", which were collected in New Verse (1925). The metre of these poems was based on syllables rather than accents, and he used the principle again in the long philosophical poem The Testament of Beauty (1929), for which he received the Order of Merit. Perhaps The Testament of Beauty is his most highly regarded work but he also wrote and also translated historic hymns, and many of these were included in Songs of

Syon (1904) and the later English Hymnal (1906). Several of Bridges' hymns and translations are still in use today.

Bridges work with the Society for Pure English (S.P.E.) was interrupted by the War but resumed in 1919. The work for the S.P.E. led to Bridges' only trip to America in 1924, during which he increased interest in the group among American scholars.

As previously mentioned his masterpiece, a long philosophical poem entitled The Testament of Beauty, was begun on Christmas Day, 1924, with fourteen lines of what he referred to as "loose Alexandrines." He set the piece aside until 1926, when the death of his daughter Margaret prompted him to resume work as a way to ease his grief. The Testament of Beauty was published in October 1929, one day after his eighty-fifth birthday and six months before his death.

A Victorian who by choice remained apart from the aesthetic movements of his day, Robert Bridges was a classicist and experimented with eighteenth-century classical forms..

On December 2nd 1929 he was pictured on the cover that week of Time Magazine

Robert Seymour Bridges' health was failing and undermined by cancer and its complications he died at his home, Chilswell, on 21 April 1930. His ashes are buried near the family cross in the churchyard of St Peter and St Paul's Church, Yattendon, Berkshire.

The cross was originally erected by Bridges in memory of his mother Harriet Elizabeth. There is also a memorial tablet to him inside the church.

Robert Seymour Bridges – A Concise Bibliography

Poetry collections
The Growth of Love (1876; 1889; 1898), a sequence of (24; 79; 69) sonnets
Prometheus the Firegiver: A Mask in the Greek Manner (1883)
Eros and Psyche: A Narrative Poem in Twelve Measures (1885; 1894), a story from the Latin of Apuleius
Shorter Poems, Books I–IV (1890)
Shorter Poems, Books I–V (1894)
New Poems (1899)
Demeter: A Mask (1905), performed 1904
Ibant Obscuri: An Experiment in the Classical Hexameter (1916), with reprint of summary of Stone's Prosody, accompanied by 'later observations & modifications'
October and Other Poems (1920)
The Tapestry: Poems (1925), in neo-Miltonic syllabics
New Verse (1926),
The Testament of Beauty (1929)

Verse drama
Nero (1885), historical tragedy; called The First Part of Nero after the publication of Nero: Part II
The Feast of Bacchus (1889); partly translated from the Heauton-Timoroumenos of Terence

Achilles in Scyros (1890), a drama in a mixed manner
Palicio (1890), a romantic drama in five acts in the Elizabethan manner
The Return of Ulysses (1890), a drama in five acts in a mixed manner
The Christian Captives (1890), a tragedy in five acts in a mixed manner; on the same subject as Calderón's El Principe Constante
The Humours of the Court (1893), a comedy in three acts; founded on Calderón's El secreto á voces and on Lope de Vega's El Perro del hortelano
Nero, Part II (1894)

Prose
Milton's Prosody, With a Chapter on Accentual Verse (1893; 1901; 1921), based on essays published in 1887 and 1889
Keats (1895)
Hymns from the Yattendon Hymnal (1899)
The Spirit of Man (1916)
Poems of Gerard Manley Hopkins (1918), edited with notes by R.B.
The Necessity of Poetry (1918)
Collected Essays, Papers, Etc. (1927–36)

www.ingramcontent.com/pod-product-compliance
Lightning Source LLC
Chambersburg PA
CBHW060102050426
42448CB00011B/2588